Fred Emerson Brooks

Battle Ballads

Fred Emerson Brooks

Battle Ballads

ISBN/EAN: 9783744652223

Printed in Europe, USA, Canada, Australia, Japan

Cover: Foto ©ninafisch / pixelio.de

More available books at **www.hansebooks.com**

BATTLE BALLADS

BY
Fred Emerson Brooks

BATTLE BALLADS.

BY

Fred Emerson Brooks.

SAN FRANCISCO:
PUBLISHED FOR THE AUTHOR.
1886.

CONTENTS.

	PAGE
Pat's Confederate Pig,	7
Grant Memorial—	
The Funeral of the Mountains,	11
Halt!	14
Crazy Vet,	16
Guns,	19
The Nation's Dead,	26
G. A. R.	35
Camp-fire,	36
Blossoms for the Brave,	37
Open the Gate!	39
The Colonel's Little Joe,	43
Blind Joe,	50
Lee at Appomattox,	53
Lee to the Confederate Flag,	54
Sherman at Shiloh,	57
Halleck's Dry Battle at Corinth,	63
By Camp-fire and Fireside,	66
Surgeon Puff!	67
Song of the Ensign,	73
The Little "Confederate,"	76
The Mutilated Soldier,	80
Potomac,	86
Independence Day—	
The First Known Yankee Notion,	99
Our Country,	103
Apostrophe to the Eagle,	112

PAT'S CONFEDERATE PIG.

When the war broke out Pat was first to enlist;
He'd fight wid shillaly or fight wid his fist.

Now Patrick was fresh from the ould, ould sod,
And carried a gun as he'd carry a hod.

He'd soon learn to shoot it, he said, without doubt,
If they'd put in the load while he'd watch it come out;

But when he had shot it he said he had ruther
Be pricked wid the one end than kicked wid the other.

His rations of whiskey he'd drink at one swig;
And never mark time but he'd end with a jig.

They went to the front: Pat thought it was hard,
The very first night to be put upon guard,

Yet he paced back and forth, out in the night air,
Rehearsing his "halt" and his "Who goes there."

"I'm to shoot at the Rebs, and aim at the heart—
But how is a stranger to tell 'em apart?"

"I'll know Mr. Rebel, the officers say,
By the clothes he has on, supposed to be gray.

Is a gentleman judged by the cut of his clothes,
As a toper is told by the tint of his nose?

"But how can I tell if he come in the dark?
Must I judge of the tree by feelin' the the bark?

I'll be sure of his wardrobe, bedad, ere I shoot!
To be the *right* man he must wear the *wrong* suit!

I think I'll surround, him the first thing I say,
Then axe him this question: Your coat, is it gray?

But I swear by the whiskey that's in my canteen
I'll not trouble him if he's *wearing the green*."

'Tis late in the night—all the camp is asleep—
When Pat hears a noise that makes his flesh creep!

Something crawls through the brush! Pat holloes out "halt!"
And "Who goes there? If you're deaf, it's your fault!"

All he hears is r-r-ruff! r-r-ruff! That sounds like a grunt—
"He's a rough sure," said Pat, "for his language is blunt—

March here and surrender me, Reb, or you die!
Come! out wid yer business! I'll bet you're a spy!"

U-g-h-w-e-e! U-g-h-w-e-e! "Holy murther! What language
  is that?
'Tis some foreign tongue, I'll be blowed!" muttered Pat.

"An officer sure—but betwixt you and me,
Is the whole army wid ye?" *U-g-h-w-e-e! U-g-h-w.e-e!*
  U-g-h-w-e-e! U-g-h-w-e-e!

"We! we!" muttered Pat; "surely that's French for *yes*
I'll capture an army! Hold, aisy—I guess

I'd better have help—so I'll call up the crowd,—
The Rebels are on us!" he cries out aloud.

"The Rebels are on us!" Out rush the whole corps,
Surrounding the wood, which they quickly search o'er,

Then sweep through the brush at a double-quick jog;
But all they can find is a dirty white hog.

They cursed till they laughed and laughed till they cried.
For rousing the army, next day Pat was tried.

"Court-martialed?" said Pat—"My offense is not big,
Why not try the army for *rousin'* the pig?

But since I've no lawyer to fix up my case
Wid fiction—I'll gi e ye the truth in its place.

He came in the night, wid a lie in his mouth,
Just like a Confederate, straight from the South.

I axed him this question, for I couldn't see:—
Are you, sir, a spy? Then he answered: We! we!

As I am a soldier, I'll ne'er dance a jig—
But he was a Rebel disguised as a pig.

I've brought into court, to confirm what I say,
These bristles, that prove he was wearin' the "gray."

'Twas all that was left me, I'm sad to relate—
The rest of the pig, sirs, you officers ate.

To speak out me moind, sure I'll die but it's true,
There's many a *pig* here that's *wearin' the blue*!!"

THE FUNERAL OF THE MOUNTAINS.

Delivered at Oakland, California, at the Grant Memorial Ceremony, August 8, 1885.

Mourn, Great McGregor, mourn! Thou youngest of
The mountains newly born; bow down thy head
And weep into the valley rivulets
Of tears. Draw 'round the close thy somber, dark
And heavy robe of pines. It is thy cloak
Of mourning and thy crape; thou hast most need
To mourn being most blessed. But yesterday
Thou wert unknown and insignificant;
To-day thou art immortal made because
Thou art the death-bed of our loved Grant,—
Because the Nation's hero made of thee
A stepping-stone to heaven.
                    Thou art become
The country's shrine, where weeping Liberty
Hath come to shed her tears. Around thy base
Is marshaled that innumerable host
Of soldiers slain in Freedom's cause, and with
Them is the captive throng in gray—with heads
Uncovered all, beneath one flag that droops
Fresh wet with heaven's tears, the dew. Those coats
Which once were blue have faded into gray;

Grave-ashes gives one color to them all.
With guns all stacked, within the silent wood
They stretch their phantom tents in bivouac weird—
A specter guard—Grand Army of the dead!
Thy cooling breeze hath kissed his fevered cheek
These long, long waiting hours so gratefully;
Thy sentry pines swayed with the fleeting pulse
And whispered undisturbingly: "All 's Well!"
When all was o'er, their wailing message went
Along the clouds, that fleecy telephone,
To Lookout Mount, whose rusty cannon's boom
Seemed like the tolling clock of destiny
Slow striking *Sixty Three.*
    For such an one
No common sepulture! Be thou his bier,
His catafalque! Let battle-mountains be
His fun'ral train! Call Lookout from the clouds,
With Mission Ridge, Ball's Bluff and Malvern Hill,
South Mountain, Champion Hill, Great Cumberland,
Pea Ridge, and those that shut in Gettysburg;
With Rural Hill and Drury's Bluff, the heights
Of Maryland and Harper's Ferry walls,
With those that frown on Shenandoah's plain;
Each hill where war hath plowed great furrows up—
Each slope with human abatis of slain—
Each mound where fiery battle-steeds have pranced,
Impatient of the smoke. E'en that small knoll
At Appomattox, where Rebellion gave

Its saber up and Slavery made her tomb;
Let heaven, muffling up her thunder drum,
Sound reveille, to summon all to this
Great funeral. In military line,
Procession make with solemn obsequies;
While ocean waves on either shore, in great
Sabaoth, *Triste Vale* chant.
     With pick
And spade think not to make thy hero's bed!
In Donelson's firm walls impregnable,
His mausoleum make—fit catacomb—
And soldier-like, wrapped in his country's flag,
There let him hold the fort for evermore.

Take shattered cannon from the battle-field,
Well moulten in hot Sumpter's crucible,
And cast a monument o'er-topping that
Of *Liberty enlightening the world;*
And on its base inscribe with sabre point—
Our Hero dead, who never battle lost,
To heaven *surrendered unconditional.*

HALT!

Delivered in connection with "The Funeral of the Mountains," at the Grant Memorial Ceremony, Oakland, Cal., Aug. 8, 1885.

High on the Nation's adamant,
  To tell to future age the story,
There Fame has chiseled "U. S. Grant,"
  And time but gilds it o'er with glory.

Round Washington doth crystalize
  Old Revolution's splendid story;
While U. S. Grant doth symbolize
  Our great Rebellion's modern glory.

When Slavery clanked her heavy chain
  'Gainst Sumpter's wall, so old and hoary,
It 'roused that spirit born to gain
  The Nation's love, a world of glory.

When Freedom tore her banner down
  To staunch the blood of heroes gory,
For aye, at Appomattox town,
  'Twas raised by thee in ten-fold glory.

Presenting arms, they wait for you,
    'Those comrades erst of field and foray;
Now standing there in grand review,
    All marshaled on the field of glory.

When by the camp-fire's told again,
    In anecdote, rebellion's story,
In lasting bivouac with your men,
    Sleep! 'neath the sentry guard of glory!

Thy name shall nerve the saber stroke,
    Whene'er through field, with banner gory,
Great soldiers chase, through battle smoke,
    Hard after fame, to die for glory.

The eagle sits with folded wing—
    Who followed thee through battles gory—
To be thy consort now, and bring
    Thy spirit to the King of Glory.

The sun shines through the window there,
    And angles beckon mandatory,
While coming down its golden stair,
    To take our hero up to glory.

Pile flowers, sweet prayers, to touch the sky!
    An offering propitiatory!
Till he, with all the host on high,
    Shall catch the perfume there in glory.

CRAZY VET.

Just stand aside thar stranger!
I reckon I'll see fair play!
For I, too, was a soldier,
Though I wore Confederate gray!
But I'll not see a veteran
Abused by swells like you,—
For four years fightin' taught me
To respect that coat of *blue!*

Abusin' a war-worn soldier,
By callin' him "Crazy Vet,"
Is a mighty poor way, I'm thinkin',
O' payin' a Nation's debt!
You say: "his head was injured
By a bit of flying shell?"
Well I've a durned good notion
To crack your skulls as well!

I want to tell ye my story:
When I joined "Stonewall Jack.,"
My mother and sister had plenty
To last 'em till I got back;

When up came "Mosby's guerillas"
And robbed 'em of all they had!
But heaven kept 'em from starvin',
By sendin' a Union lad!

The advance of the Yankee army,
Brought my home within their lines;
And that young colonel's camp-fire
Was just beneath our pines!
He filled my mother's larder
With the best he had in store!
And what with his foragin' soldiers,
The house could hold no more!

When I came home, this story
Was told me, again and again;
While tears of regret came often,
To think I had fought such men!
But now I'm worth my thousands,
And looking for colonel Grace!
And after months o' sarchin'
I'm told he's about this place!

I'd like ye to help me find him:—
Great Scott! What's that ye say!
This is the man I'm seekin'
That you've tormented that way?

To send you home to the Devil,
Would be treatin' you far too well!
I would—but that the "new version"
Explodes the old fashioned *hell*!

No! no! I begs forgivness—
I'm rather rough in my way—
God bless you for this reunion
Between the "blue and the gray!"
I'll seek some skillfull surgeon
And repair the ill that's done;
Then take him back to my mother,
Who calls him her *blue-coat son.*

And I don't mind yer knowin'
I've got a sister fair,—
A wealth of love in her bosom—
A wealth of gold in her hair—
And *these two*—wall, no matter!
Just you say "*Crazy Vet*"
*And I'll start another Rebellion
And clean out you Yanks, you bet!"*

GUNS.

Hear the cracking of the rifle,
Hear the ball, that leaden trifle,
    Whizzing by !
Whizzing by ? O, that will do,
But suppose it should go through ?
    Would we die ?

O, 'tis such a fatal skill,
Where each ball is meant to kill —
    Where 'tis known,
That for every missile borne,
Some frail uniform is torn,
Wife or mother left to mourn,
    All alone.

'Tis the nation's firm command !
It is done to save the land,
    And the slave !
Ah ! but there's another reason,
No strange banner flaunting treason,
    Here may wave !

Swift from musket's polished steel,
Comes the message: woe or weal,
    Mostly woe;
Soldiers shoot as if they meant it,
Bullet comes as if Death sent it,
    From the foe.

From its course, nor turns nor trends;
Makes a wound no surgeon mends,
    And a flood!
Soldier drops from out the ranks,
Dearly earns the nation's thanks,
    With his blood.

And that bayonet you know, sir,
Is for argument much closer,
    Than before;
While each point is such debate,
Seals some noble fellow's fate,
    Evermore.

That great question is decided—
Nation shall not be divided!
    Look, how pale
Are those cheeks that once were ruddy,
While the blue-coats, torn and bloody,
    Tell the tale.

What is that unearthly rattling?
That's another gun, by Gatling;
    How it c-r-a-c-k-s!
'Tis no birthday of the nation!
This is Death's own celebration!
    Firing packs

Of great crackers! Turn the crank,
Horrors rattle out in flank,
    Sum untold!
Aimed at yonder gray battalion,
Where fate rides a fretting stallion,
    Uncontrolled.

There are guns that speak much louder;
There are guns that use more powder,
    Stronger death.
Belching fire across the way,
Like volcanoes in full play!
    Deadly breath!

From yon atmosphere of smoke,
Some artillerist's keen stroke
    Hath cut down
Swath on swath, that doth betoken,
Mother-hearts will soon be broken,
    In the town.

Had he seen that wife's hot tears;
Known the grief to last for years—
    Widowhood !
He'd have turned away that gun ;
He'd have left that mother's son,
    Where he stood.

Polished brass gleams in the sun,
When the day's red work is done !
    And the lawn
Is much redder where they fall :
At next morning's dread roll call
    They are gone.

Dropping in another quarter,
From volcanic mouth of mortar,
    Meteors fall !
O ! that most destructive shell,
Bit of concentrated hell,
    In a ball.

How the cannon boom ! and boom !
Hoarsly shouting, room ! make room !
How they sing of sudden doom—
    Such a tune !
How the round-shot seem to roll
On some unsuspecing soul—
    All too soon.

Playing skittles through the air;
Making always *strike* or *spare*
  As they're bowled!
Like a ball hurled down death's alley,
At the ten-pins in the valley,
  Manifold.

Do they ape that ancient flood;
Letting out so much choice blood
  In the dust?
Will't corrode chains that enthrall,
Or make slavery's shackles fall!
  By its rust?

Were each drop of blood a dime,
All the slaves in southern clime
  Could be bought!
Buying slaves to set them free,
Does not crush out slavery!
  It must be fought.

Blood's cement, though 'tis not coin,
And will severed nation join;
  Well it might!
While rebellion is a thing,
That on battles smoky wing,
  Must take flight.

Do you want that little spot,
Where the fort stands reeking hot,
    'Round the city?
Must you go and batter down
Those great walls and half the town?
    What a pity!

Should some earthquake come at night,
Swallow city out of sight;
    Men would say:
"What a sad and awful fate;
Like the horrors they relate
    Of Pompeii."

Yet those guns keep plowing graves,
And keep filling them with braves;
    While their ghosts
Stand in faded "blue" and "gray,"
Marshaled all in dumb array—
    Silent hosts.

Put a fuse into some crater!
Blow mankind to its Creator—
    Pell-mell!
Blow the widow and the weeper!
And the orphan and the sleeper!
Blow the world unto its keeper—
    'Tis a shell!!

What is all this fighting for?
Why will mankind go to war,
    And invent
Engines deadly, more and most,
Just to slaughter greater host?
    Sentiment!
    Government!!

Watch the farmer at his toil,
Where great gun-wheels plowed the soil;
    Flowers blooming!
'Tis much better occupation
'Tis far better for the nation
    Than guns booming.

THE NATION'S DEAD.

Delivered at Oakland, California, Memorial Day, 1885.

America's sleeping
In the arms of the ocean :
Those arms so long and bare,
Reaching out every where,
Guarding the Nation there
Sleeping.

Like a mother's devotion
These arms of old ocean
Their watch-guard are keeping;
But soon there'll be weeping.

Fond mother with arms so strong,
For foes been looking long,
For foes been looking wrong.
Looking abroad for them—
Thy foe 's within.

Thy foe is slavery,
Gotten of knavery,
'T will take all thy bravery
To put it down.

List to the dreadful din,
Hoarse cannon thundering;
Learn that thy foe's within,
Stand not there wondering.

A new flag is flying,
The old flag is lying
Trailed in the dust,
While brave men are dying,
Who had it in trust.

Hark to the thundering gun,
Right here in 'sixty-one
At Sumpter's wall.
Still it keeps rumbling,
While Sumpter keeps tumbling:
'Tis a battle, that's all.

Quick! to thy nation haste!
There's now no time to waste!
Call out thy sons!

Already they're arming,
They're leaving their farming
And taking their guns;
Fathers and cousins,
Brothers and sons.

Look at the host of them;
Hear the proud boast of them;
Coming from most of them,
Not to return
Till Rebellion is ended,
The Union defended,
The North and South blended,
Then to return !

Infantry, cavalry,
Flying artillery;
Best blood of chivalry;
Drums beating reveille !
The trumpet is sounding.
The hills are resounding,
The war-horse is bounding,
Over the plain !
To battle they're rushing,
Their pale cheeks are flushing,
Their blood 'gins to burn,
From the field whence they're rushing
Will they ever return ?

Like corn from the crushing,
All broken return—
Heart's blood set a-gushing
Can never return.

But that is no matter;
Their sabers still clatter,
As onward they go.
That saber—what matters it,
Though an enemy batters it,
Though their own blood spatters it,
Still onward they go.

The nation's applauding,
The women all lauding
Their valor, tis true—
But no woman's flattery
E'er took a battery,
Give valor its due!

They return—but how few,
Whilst the sod and the dew
Covers the dead—
Covers the rest of them;
Covers the blest of them;
Some of the best of them—
Hallowed dead.

They send back no token
To hearts that are broken;
They died, and unspoken,
With mutterings broken,
Their good-bye was said.

Day after day, for them,
Women may pray for them,
Naught they can say for them,
Alters their doom.

They did with valor vie,
They did their valor try;
No one can tell us why
They were marked out to die,
Yet under cloud and sky,
Under the sod they lie,
Where daisies bloom.

Women may weep for them,
Night vigils keep for them,
They'll come no more.
In earth's bosom deep for them
There's eternal sleep for them,
Forevermore!

The nation but yesterday, met to debate
With bayonet point the question great:

Resolved: The black man no longer shall be
A slave, in the land where the rest are free.

The debate caused the nation a world of fears
And wives and mothers an ocean of tears.

But the stamp of the war-horse created the shock
That broke the shackles and shattered the lock.

The question was settled, and so shall remain,
And our only regret is the loss of the slain.

The guns are all stacked; the sentry sleeps,
But the camp-fire burns which glory keeps,

While they're waiting the roll-call over head,
That slumb'ring army—the nation's dead.

Oh, what a fearful storm was that,
That deadly leaden rain.
O, what a dreadful sight was that,
The dying and the slain.

The phantom sexton moved about,
Though not a word he said,
But put his fatal mark upon
The dying and the dead.

Then came the phantom grave-men,
With lantern, pick and spade;
They heard the sexton's dumb command
And silently obeyed.

And when their spectral work was done
And crosses planted there,
These phantom grave-men filed away
And vanished—anywhere.

We find some graves with name and date,
While others seem forgot,
With nothing but a nameless cross
To mark the hallowed spot.

Red war did never shed such blood,
Nor braver men inter;
While valor never was embalmed
In better sepulcher.

The strife is ended, and a score
Of years have passed away;
The nation's covered up its dead,
Their bodies turned to clay.

In life they fought with bitterest hate!
The fiercest foes 'tis true;
Death makes them friends—no matter now,
Which coat was "gray," which "blue."

They fought to take each other's life,
There was no other way;
While now there's many a self same grave
Holds both the "blue" and "gray."

Both coats are of one color now;
The grave brings quick decay;
Each coat is turned to ashes now,
Each coat is colored "gray."

The fresh green grass, like bayonet blades,
Guards them all these years,
'Tis always wet with heaven's dew,
And oft with women's tears.

And when we measure all the tears,
And count the lives so lost,
We wonder if the black man knows
Just what his freedom cost.

The negro—does he think, alone,
He caused this war, I wonder?
'Twas not the slave, but slavery
Near cut this land asunder.

That fact alone aroused the brave
And fired each patriot heart,
No power on earth, they stoutly swore,
Shall tear that flag apart!

We wonder, when we count the cost,
And reckon every grave,

Why nations will enrich their soil
With ashes of their brave.

No wonder that we love that flag!
Remembering what we paid—
No wonder that we deck the graves
That stopped the slavery trade.

The country o'er, they lie asleep,
In many a sacred spot;
While our fresh flowers, fresh tears, proclaim
They'll never be forgot.

The great rebellion sent its bier,
With friend, with kin and kith;
War sent us soldiers' graves out here,
Heaven, flowers to deck them with.

God bless the sacrifice they made,
They died for Uncle Sam;
Their names we'll keep for ever more,
Fresh in memoriam.

There's one green mantle covers both.
They're sleeping there like brothers;
They'll sleep there till the judgment day,
Until God calls both "blue" and "gray,"
Because they died for others.

G. A. R.

Sung at 20th National Encampment of G. A. R., at San Francisco, 1886.

Our God shall guard the land we love,
Where dwells the eagle and the dove;
Where none are warriors by trade.
But all are soldiers ready made.

REFRAIN.

All hail our eagle soaring high,
Trailing our banner through the sky,
Emblazoned on each crimson bar
That royal title—G. A. R.

This nation ever shall revere
Its valorous Union volunteer,
Whose flashing steel o'erwhelmed the foe
That sought the Union's overthrow.

He guards his flag when foes assail,
As mountain crag defies the gale;
When he gives 'way, just where he stood
You'll find his body and his blood.

Should foreign foe sound war's alarms,
A myriad freemen rush to arms;
No power defeats the man of toil,
Who fights for home and his own soil.

CAMP-FIRE.

Sung at 20th National Encampment of G. A. R., at San Francisco, 1886.

Potomac's great army is gathering once more
"Ohio" and famed "Tennessee"
The "Cumberland";—all from the sea or the shore,
To join in our grand jubilee.

REFRAIN.

Come, rally 'round the Camp-fire, boys,
Just as you did in "Sixty-one";
To swell our happy throng,
Bring all the boys along,
But leave at home the sabre and the gun.

See yon mighty host! Sherman rides in the van,
From "Georgia" they're tramping along;
Fast marching this way with the great Iron-man,
All singing our Camp-fire song.

From that famous ride into Winchester town,
To where he made *Lee* stand at bay,
Whenever Phil Sheridan's horsemen came down
The "*Rebs.*" had to scamper away.

And here's to brave comrades, remembered with love,
Who hold their re-union on high
With *Grant* and the rest, 'round the Camp-fires above—
Those beautiful stars in the sky.

BLOSSOMS FOR THE BRAVE

Delivered at San Francisco, at the Memorial Day Ceremony, May 30, 1886.

We think of you as brave and true
    Grand army of the dead;
You are asleep 'neath sod and dew,
    Grand army of the dead;
Thou who did'st the nation save,
Here we come to deck thy grave,
Scattering blossoms on the brave,
    Grand army of the dead.

No more ye hear the cannon boom,
    Grand army of the dead;
Your flag is floating o'er your tomb,
    Grand army of the dead;
Here we come with flowers to-day,
Here our orisons we say,
Sleep ye there till judgment day,
    Grand army of the dead.

Your bivouac tent is grassy knoll,
    Grand army of the dead;
Eternal rest your long parole,
    Grand army of the dead.

Death-white lips, the blood-red hue,
Staining every blouse of blue,
Show the nation's debt to you,
    Grand army of the dead.

Comrades, uncover! Make salute!!
    Grand army of the dead.
Sweet messengers these flowers mute,
    Grand army of the dead.
Precious blood where valor dies;
Hallowed spot where patriot lies;
Gateway up to paradise,
    Grand army of the dead.

OPEN THE GATE!

Delivered at the Hancock Memorial, San Francisco, Feb. 28, 1886.

Hard by the nation's temple of Fame,
Where sleep the great, in deed and name,
Liberty strides with solemn tread,
Eternal guard of the treasured dead.
Outside on tessellated floor,
Outside the walls with golden door,
Her sentry step the nation hears,
In measured beat through waiting years;
To watch the gate, her constant care,
That only the great may enter there.

From Governor's Island cannons boom,
Thus death salutes the fallen plume;
The fortress flag is lowered half,
And drooping, clings the barren staff;
Sword, glory hilted, laid aside;
The silent barge floats down the tide;
Down to the Nation's temple of fame,
The speechless helmsman guides the prame.

The barge is moored at Fame's green isle,
The catafalque removed the while—
Brave soldiers, craped, with arms reverse,
Upon their shoulders—human hearse—
With muffled drum and mournful air,
The casket of their chieftain bear.
Up that same path where late they came,
Up to the Nation's temple of fame.

The Goddess sees the solemn train,
And o'er the music's sad refrain
Cries to the mourning leaders—Stay !
Set down the corse ! what seek ye, pray ?
Do ye not know, who bear the bier,
None but the great may enter here ?
And who is this for whom ye claim
Eternal rest in temple of fame ?

This is the fame our hero has :
At Churubusco, Contreras,
A youthful soldier awed the foe,
In stubborn war with Mexico ;
At San Antonio 'twas he
Who bore the palm of bravery.
Then open the gate to him who came
Up, step by step, to temple of fame ;

Our Captain heard, in sixty-one,
War's fierce alarm from Sumpter's gun;
At Williamsburg, the soldiers say,
'Twas his fierce charge that won the day.
South Mountain, with Antietam's field,
Proved him a soldier would not yield,
Deeds stalwart, fitting stalwart frame,
Earn him the right to temple of fame.

At Golding's Farm and Garnett's Hill;
At Fredericksburg and Chancellorsville;
At Savage Station, Marye's Height,
We found him in the hottest fight.
At Spottsylvania, Wilderness,
Cold Harbor, Petersburg, no less:
These give our hero lasting name!
Then open the gate to temple of fame.

'Twas he held Cemetery Ridge,
That made for victory a bridge
To breast rebellion's rushing tide.
When he checked Longstreet's madd'ning ride
On doubtful field, he won by far
The grandest victory of the War,
And gave to Gettysburg a name
That wins his right to temple of fame.

The casket lies uncovered there ;
That noble face, the silvered hair,
Proclaim to all, in accents mute,
Great virtue, rarer attribute
Than tales of valor you may hear—
Great Goddess, bid us raise the bier,
And to this one of spotless name
Pray ope the gate, Warden of fame.

This door is only for the great,
Whose deeds we would perpetuate;
Twice has it opened inthe year—
For Grant's and for Mc Clellan's bier;
And now again, the Nation saith:
As once in life, so e'en in death,
'Tis fit that he should follow Grant,
Like a true soldier, militant;
And now the Goddess speaks once more,
As slowly swings the golden door ;
To all the world I now proclaim,
Hancock shall hawe eternal fame.

THE COLONEL'S LITTLE JOE.

When both lines lay
Like stags at bay,
In the days of "Sixty-one,"
A little scamp
Came into camp,
And asked to carry a gun!

My little man,
I doubt if you can
Hold up a gun so large!
You'd die of fright,
Before the fight,
Or ere we came to charge!

With face so grave
He said: "I'm brave!
And couldn't I beat the drum?
For I've no pa!
And I've no ma!
Or else I wouldn't have come!"

'Tis a risk you take—
But a " marker " you'd make,
To straighten the columns by !
You'd have to stand,
Small flag in hand,
My lad, where the bullets fly !

" My name is Joe !
I'd have you know
I've got a coat of blue !
But what if I got
An extra shot
The *Rebs.* had aimed at you?"

'Twould be a shame !
I'd feel to blame,
If you should die for me !
So bright a lad,
With lot so sad,
A better fate should see !

'Tis strange, indeed,
That I should heed
Your tale—and hear it through !
And stranger still,
My heart should fill
With such a love for you !

But in your face
A look I trace—
So like my angel boy!
Who died one day
In early May,
'Way back in Illinois.

I have a wife,
Dear as my life;
And when the war is done,
You shall fall heir
To that vacant chair,
And be to us a son!

"I have not heard
A pleasant word,
Save yours, for many a day!"
Joe ceased to speak!
But down his cheek
Ran words he could not say.

Then in the tent
The Colonel bent,
And kissed the golden hair!
His epaulette
With tears grew wet—
That Joe was dropping there.

What soldiers prize
They idolize,
As every one may know!
And little blame
That soon they came
To worship Colonel's Joe.

Joe loved to ride
By the Colonel's side,
And hear the soldiers laugh!
He'd look austere,
When they would cheer
The Colonel *and his staff!*

No one can know
How little Joe
Crept in the Colonel's heart;
Together thrown—
Down there alone—
From other loves apart!

In pleasant spot,
The soldier's lot
Is one without a care;
But what a change,
When, at short range—
Death flanks him every where!!

When that brigade,
By fierce charge, made
Each field a slaughter pen !
    Joe was the first
    To quench the thirst,
And succor wounded men.

    In rain of hell,
    Which often fell
From those war-clouds of woe,
    'Twas strange that not
    A single shot
Struck Colonel or his Joe !

    There's much to abhor
    In open war !
But in the "Sharpshooter's" aim—
    That cowardly blow
    From a secret foe—
There lies a *Nation's shame* !

    True hunters blush
    To hide in brush,
And shoot the couching stag !
    But hidden aim
    At *human* game
Disgraces any flag ! !

The tent was laid
Beneath the shade
Of spreading hemlock tree;
Where the Colonel sat,
For a little chat
With Joe, upon his knee!

When a rifle shot
From yonder spot—
Where lurked a hidden foe—
On death intent.
For the Colonel meant,
Stopped short in the breast of Joe!

The Colonel—dumb—
With grief o'ercome,
Spoke not in his despair!
But little Joe
Said: "I will go,
And wait for you, *up there!*"

"Weep not!" he said;
"But when I'm dead—
And sleep as soldiers do—
Tell *her* I got
That extra shot
The "Rebs" had aimed at you!"

Bearing that smile,
That stays a while,
When soul and body part;
With drooping head,
Poor Joe lay, dead,
Upon the Colonel's heart.

They made a grave
For the little brave,
Where angels hov'ring low,
Stepped from the cloud,
On " Lookout," proud,
And took up Little Joe!

BLIND JOE.

Joe Parsons was brave, but somewhat gruff;
A noted wag and rather tough!
'Twas on Antietam's field he lay,
With both his eyes clean shot away.

"I'm in a fix," he said, "and fear
My eyes have gone and left me here!
I have no eyes to close in sleep,
And for their loss no eyes to weep!

I'd walk about, but do not know,
Without my sight, which way to go
Among the dead, unless I'm shown!"
At length he hears a soldier groan.

"Hello thar, stranger! How de do!
I'm a 'Yank'! Pray, who are you?
Wal, I'm a 'Reb,' and wear the gray!
And both my legs are shot away!

Old Butternut, come here to me!
For I am blind and cannot see!
How like derned fools you Yankees talk!
I've lost my legs! How can I walk?

All right, old pal, just hold your own,
And guide me by that dismal groan
Till I can grope my way to you,
Then we'll resolve what's best to do.

'Tis legs you need and eyes I lack!
So I'll just tote you on my back!
If you can somehow sit astride,
I'll be the beast and let you ride;

But drive me gently with a *chirrup,*
For you've no feet and I've no stirrup;
And bear in mind, you must not fool
E'en with a blind, old, army mule.

But understand, 'Old Porcupine,'
You guide me to the 'Union' line."
The "Reb." assents, with blandishment,
But guides him to *Confederate* tent.

"What have we here, a Yankee spy?"
The Colonel asks, "Then let him die!"
But nothing daunted, out speaks Joe:
"The blind man knows not friend from foe!

My presence here no pardon begs;
He is the *spy*, I'm but the *legs!*
To speak a little plainer, 'boss,'
He is the man!   I'm but the *hoss*,

Or beast, perhaps, of lower class;
In playing *horse* I've proved an *ass!*
An error, Colonel, of the mind,
Which pray excuse, since I am blind;
I chose the *Devil* for my *pal*,
Who proves a *Rebel General!*

LEE AT APPOMATTOX.

*Delivered at Anniversary of Appomattox Post, G. A. R.,
Oakland, Cal., 1886.*

At Appomattox, when the war was done,
Each soldier leaning on his silent gun,

Stood Robert Lee, upon that famous knoll,
And bade his army sign the long parole.

Thus victory clasped hands with sore defeat,
And made secession henceforth obsolete!

The white-haired chieftain keenly felt the stroke,
And to his yielding army thus he spoke:

"Brave comrades, mine, of many a well-fought field,
Scarred veterans, the time has come to yield!

The fates declare our bleeding cause is lost,
And prove rebellion dear at any cost!

Red war has rolled its devastating flood,
And left a Nation floundering in its blood!"

LEE TO THE CONFEDERATE FLAG.

(Read as part of previous poem.)

   Pull down Rebellion's flag!
Once proudly waved from battlement and fort,
While millions cheered and thousands gave support,
    'Tis now a useless rag,
And droops in token of its own defeat,
And humbly doth its honored victor meet.

   The edict has been said:
This country brooks no standard but its own!
Let this one live in memory alone!
    Like its defenders dead
It must lie buried in the nation's dust!
'Tis never what we would but what we must!

   Emblem of mortal strife—
Its stripes were cut out by the saber blade;
In human blood 'twas dyed, in discord made;
    And borne where war was rife
In constant battle smoke without surcease;
It never knew the gentle breath of peace!

Flag of the bleeding South—
How many noble souls have rushed to death,
And said their final prayer in gasping breath,
    With dry and parched mouth,
Through their vain faith in thee! What thy return?
Defeat! Most bitter dregs in broken urn.

    Brave men, with coats of blue—
Behold these gray battalions battle-worn!
Behold their flag in smoke of battle torn!
    This work was done by you!
Go, count the slain! On every field they lie!
Opinions live, while their defenders die!

    I've heard an army cheer
That flag, and shout above the cannon's roar,
And rushing, pile their dead up by the score
    Like grain sheaves, tier on tier;
And make in one short hour a world of woe,
To wrest a worthless standard from the foe!

    Let no more blood be shed!
Pull down that flag! 'Tis no disgrace to yield—
Our father's flag is master of the field!
    Go, spread it o'er the dead,
And know: He justly feels th'avenging rod
Who fights against his country and his God!

'Tis painful to return
To ruined homes, where sit fond mothers, wives,
In useless tears, bewailing wasted lives;
  And meekly bid them learn
That nevermore on high with martial strain
Shall slavery's flag cut freedom's breeze in twain.

  A generous victor saith :
Lay down your guns—no more shout war's alarm;
Let each man keep his horse to till his farm
  And plow the field of death !
Down in the dust let treason's banner drag,
And homeward proudly bear your country's flag.

  The three-barred flag came down—
Presumptuous cause of fratricidal war—
The *stars and stripes* they raised, then shouted for;
  Then back through field and town,
As proudly as the victors, bore it thence,
To be the first to die in its defence.

SHERMAN AT SHILOH.

The Shiloh church was closed that Sabbath morn:
Like dove of peace with folded wing, forlorn—

Hoarse war profane had hushed its sacred song:
The congregation many thousand strong,

Their dusky forms outside in morn's dull light,
Had come there, not to worship, but to fight.

Hard by the church, fit metal for the van,
Renowned Tecumseh stands: the *Iron man !*

The river, with its branches, guards three sides,
While down the fourth the Rebel army strides,

As springs the furious lion from his lair:—
To stop the onslaught fierce, was Sherman there,

As some great bluffs are set by God's decree,
To stop the useless fury of the sea.—

As lesser rocks are by the tide o'erwhelmed,
Sinks Prentiss down—and like a ship unhelmed,

Yonder brave Stuart flounders in the flood;
While back, McClernand wades a tide of blood.

With force divided, Grant must wait for Buell:
Grant knew there was no heat in scattered fuel;

But must obey *great* Halleck's strange commands,
As one who fights with shackles on his hands.

No error may be scored against that man
Who fights a battle on another's plan.

At early morn Grant hears the battle's roar,
So fiercely Johnson batters at his door.

"To horse!" he cries—Savannah, miles away
To South he leaves, swift riding to the fray.

As rising tide o'erwhelms the swaying reeds,
O'erborne, the wavering army slow recedes;

They catch the glint of yonder shoulder-star
'Our Chieftain comes! The man with a cigar!!'

The words pass on, fast swelling into cheers!
Sad requiem in fallen Johnson's ears.

Grant's orders *fly !* Along the front he flies !
Grant smokes!—the battle smokes, e'en to the skies.

Now Beauregard in frenzy flies the field !
But for the *Iron man* who will not yield

He'd drive those Yanks into the Tennessee;
But old Tecumseh says: '*It shall not be.*'

As some great hulk the waves have driven ashore,
Stops where their combined fury drives no more :

Or wounded boar, by dogs o'ermatched, at bay—
Recedes, but still is master of the day.

Another stand he makes when one is lost,
By Rebels purchased at too great a cost.

All heedless rides he through that musket hail,
As one who wears a coat of charméd mail.

Horse after horse beneath this rider falls,
Great marvel hungry death no closer calls.

Oft, courting danger as a welcome guest,
This Sabbath day is not his day of rest.

The Rebels mass to catch him on the flank:
A well-placed batt'ry lays the solid rank

As on wet fields you've seen the storm-lodged grain:
To silence it charge cavalry in vain,

For veteran musketry stand in their track,
And make those horses riderless turn back !

The battle theirs, by carrying that ravine !
But this great movement Grant has long foreseen ;

His sleeping monsters on the river there
Thunder their tumult on the Sabbath air ;

Up that ravine those gunboats bowl the shell:—
"Retreat ! 'Tis Grant's command ! Make room ! !" they yell

And those who dare this edict disobey
Go down like human tenpins, bowled away.

The lingering Nelson, Grant draws up in form ;
Then issues forth that *cold " Galena "* storm.

'Tis not in human power to stand such fire ;
The bugle sounds, they sullenly retire.

And as those shattered ranks move out of sight
Red battle slinks away into the night;

Grim darkness draws her mantle overhead,
And covers up the living and the dead.

The river gunboats, still maintaining fight,
With arching shell light up the dome of night;

Great screaming meteors hurled through black space,
Or comets fleet, engaged in midnight race.

There float black gunboats in the clouds as well,
That answer back with just as deadly shell;

God's lightning comes down zigzag to the floor;
Man's fatal lightning whizzes, circling o'er:

Both thunderbolts have set the woods on fire;
A bivouac light at once, and funeral pyre:

Man's mimic thunder vies with God's o'erhead,
In that great midnight battle o'er the dead.

The crystal bullets fall—the dead are drenched;
Great mercy 'tis, for wounded thirst is quenched.

One shudders at a dead man in the way;
But here are thousands dead, in blue and gray.

The living sleep beside them in the rain:
God's tears co-mingle with the crimson stain.

Far back are living, wounded, dead and all;
Black darkness serves for blanket and for pall.

With Buell's reinforcements well in hand;
Through darkness rides the chief to each command

With special orders: "At to-morrow's light
Let all advance in one o'erwhelming fight."

Then lies he down, like others, in the storm,
On the wet earth—a blanket wraps his form:

He dreams of retribution in the morn!
He hears *retreat* sound from their bugle horn!

He sees his brave battalions beat them down,
While Buell sweeps them back to Corinth town.

With *right* and *might* was victory supreme!
There sometimes is a truth wrapped in a dream.

HALLECK'S DRY BATTLE AT CORINTH.

Halleck put GRANT in disgrace:
Halleck put Smith in his place;
His wound was the sting of an adder:
Halleck drops down to obscurity;
Halleck's name goes to futurity
  As that of a man of cant,
   Who labored to ruin Grant:
He stood at the top of the ladder,
  Unworthy of mentton,
   His constant attention—
Instead of putting down slavery—
  Was the man who clung
   To a lower rung:
That compound of genius and bravery.

Halleck, the great martinet,
Halleck, fame's blank silhouette,
Could *not* shake this Grant from the ladder:
  Donaldson, Shiloh, Iuka,
   Corinth, Vicksburg, Chatanooga;
Such strides the great hero took,
No wonder fame's stepladder shook!

Then Halleck grew wiser and sadder:
So great was the shaking
He fell, quickly breaking
That bubble: his great reputation;
While up went the banner
Along with the " *Tanner,*"
A fortunate change for the nation.

After the battle of Shiloh,
Halleck came down for a while-O,
This pompous commander-in-chief:
Halleck, with tactics so wonderful
Halleck, with strategy blunderful;
His advance was a slow retard
When following Beauregard :
In six weeks—'tis past all belief—
He marched fifteen miles—
All history smiles—
His marching was unprecedented;
Then sat himself down
Before " Corinth " town
With *seventy thousand*—contented.

There he sat, sucking his thumb,
Fearing the Rebels might come:
Those Rebels were marching away;
Humor like this was outrageous:
Halleck at length grew courageous;

Assuming a terrible frown,
He marched on that vacated town—
He marched in fierce battle array!
Bravely withstood the sun!
Captured each "*wooden gun*"!
The chickens—some stray, starving cattle—
The mice and the spiders—
Those Rebel abiders
At Corinth!—Great Halleck's *dry-battle!*

Halleck, recalled in disgrace,
Tendered "*quartermaster*" his place:
He wanted it filled with renown—
Deeming his late *army-butler*
A soldier much fitter and "*subtler.*"
Fame sets Halleck alone
Squat on a pedestal stone:
The soldier who captured a town,
With a smatt'ring of mud,
But no spatt'ring of blood:
A world-renowned *wooden-gun* victory;
While gossips still tattle
Of Halleck's *dry-battle*
At Corinth: His great valedictory.

BY CAMP-FIRE AND FIRESIDE.

That night by the camp-fire soldiers slept ;
    Some dreamed of home,—some prayed !
Now for themselves, and now for the nation :
    They knew the battle was laid
And blood must be poured to make libation,
    And soldier's honor be kept.

That night by the fireside mothers wept
    For loved ones gone : All prayed—
Now for their boys, and now for the natión ;
    While hope and fear they weighed,—
And life and death in the calculation
    With equal chances crept.

The Camp-fire is out and honor kept ;
    God spared not all who prayed ;
For some must die to save the nation,
    If saved by the saber blade !
And muscles quiver their little duration,
    And bleed till the soul has slept.

The fireside is brigbt, and some have crept
    Into those arms that prayed ;
While some sleep 'neath the grass of the nation
    In death's long ambuscade ;
And he whose blood came in perspiration
    This lesser sacrifice kept.

SURGEON PUFF!

They called him Doc. Bravado!
He hailed from Colorado;
As fine a looking surgeon as could be;
He wore his hair like Custer,
But was so full of bluster
They christened him "The brag," and used a D——

While 'round the camp-fire toasting
His shins, and proudly boasting,
This crowing gascon seemed a braggart arch;
Well puffed up with pretensions,
Would strut in grand dimensions,
And ride up in the van when on the march.

His skill no soldier doubted—
But all his valor flouted,
Believing him so cowardly at heart,
The smoke of the first battle,
And noise of musket rattle
Would make him shake with fear and fall apart.

They all were heard remarking:
"A dog so fond of barking
Would never close his mouth to take a bite";
And so they planned to scare him,
In ambush to ensnare him,
And playing Rebels, frighten him that night.

And so they lay in waiting—
This Surgeon Puff berating;
And over his chagrin had many a laugh!
And while in this sequester
The regimental jester
Read them an ante-mortem epitaph!

"Here lies Surgeon Bravado,
Who hailed from Colorado!
He would have whipped the Rebels all alone,
But that he died of fear—
So, Rebels come not near!
There's danger even in each rattling bone."

And when they heard him nearing
They yelled to split his hearing!
Instead of running, he began to shout:
"Here are the Rebels, d———n 'em!"
Then he began to lamm 'em—
And wounding three, put all the rest to rout!

THE BATTLE MARCH:
OR, THE GREEN COUNTRY COUSIN.

They had not seen her for years,
That rich but green, country cousin;
And hence their numerous fears
Increased like a baker's dozen;
Because she wrote she'd be down
Just after her graduation;
Which filled these cousins in town
With fear and great purturbation.

"She's awkward as any old crow;
Will dress in such country fashion,
And drawl through her nose, I know,
To set a saint in a passion."
"Your uncle is rich," answered aunt,
And 'twill not do to refuse her,
For ask a delay—we can't!
We'll trust each guest will excuse her!

Just think of our great musicale,
With each bidden guest distinguished,
Disgraced by a green, country 'gal,'
Who can't be put down nor extinguished.

That new piece of music by Balse,
In manuscript of composer,
She'll match with old-fashioned waltz,
If some one chance to propose her."

The cousin arriving—came down
When all the guests had assembled;
While aunt's long face wore a frown,
Not knowing the girl had dissembled.
Chagrin was so plainly seen,
While emphasis helped construction;
" A country cousin—Miss Green ! "
Completed her introduction.

A smile crept o'er that sweet face
At sight of those simpers and gushes;
A fresh rose nodded with grace
Amidst artificial blushes;
She caught the composer's keen eye,
And bright grew their conversation;
While talent and beauty ran high,
And Cupid found new occupation.

'Twas time for the new march, grand;
The author begged leave to delay it—
Pretending a very weak hand—
"Unless some kind guest would play it."

While most were ambitious to try
This difficult piece, in construction,
Each one resigned, with a sigh,
Before she was through th'introduction.

Our friend glanced over the piece,
Then played with artistic precision;
And mockery found its surcease,
While melody hushed their derision:
They heard the roll of the drum!
Great volleys of musketry rattle!
The galloping cavalry come!
Then felt the shock of the battle!

The waver, the rout, the retreat!
Great captains grasping at glory!
With victory chasing defeat
Hard over the battle field gory!
They heard the boom of the gun!
And almost saw the hot flashes!
And when the battle was done
Heard Slavery groan in the ashes!

And then they came back again!
Back through the dead and the dying!
That tramp of victorious men!
With banner of freedom still flying!

Then tramp, tramp, tramp in the street!
That home-coming, scarred and broken!
Embraces and cheers to greet,
And tears where naught came but a *token!*

They all applauded with zest;
Amazed at her wonderful playing!
Since genius had gone through the test
Triumphant, she could not help saying:
"Until one's worth may be seen
Be more discreet in your greeting!
Some apples are ripe while green,
And some, though ripe, not worth eating!"

SONG OF THE ENSIGN.

Here on the brink of battle
I fondly kiss each fold ;
For yonder musket rattle
My destiny may hold !
    Dear Flag !

Thou ever precious banner,
Beloved of all the free ;
The soldier in this manner
Shows love—he dies for thee !
    Dear Flag !

What citizen-devotion
Can ever equal be
To that great soldier-notion—
Idolatry of thee !
    Dear Flag !

Thou'rt not unlike the others,
But only better made ;
For sweethearts, sisters, mothers
Stitched in each silken shade !
    Dear Flag !

In prayer they clasp those fingers;
In prayer they bend the knee ;
Their blessing 'round thee lingers;
I kiss them, kissing thee !
  Dear Flag !

I kiss them for my fellows,
So soon to cast the lot !
For Fate works at the bellows !
The forge will soon be hot !
  Dear Flag !

And Freedom's breeze is kissing,
Upon thy silken scroll,
Those names to be marked missing,
When next they call the roll !
  Dear Flag !

'Tis well we can not read them :—
Enough to say adieu
Whenever death shall need them :—
Perhaps my name's there, too !
  Dear Flag !

Our regiment is standing
In battle's dumb array—
And waits but the commanding,
To dash into the fray !—
  Dear Flag !

Like fierce stampede of cattle,
We'll rush where foe besets !
Right in the teeth of battle :
Those glistening bayonets !
    Dear Flag !

And I'm the one to bear thee !
The one to lead the way !
The God of battles spare me,
To bring thee back to-day !
    Dear Flag !

If I shall fall in battle,
Why, thou wilt be my shroud,
When muffled drum shall rattle
Its anthem to the cloud !
    Dear Flag !

Then, by the clod and clover !
Shut out from blue on high !
Thy blue sky shall be over !
Thy bright stars ever nigh !
    Dear Flag !

THE LITTLE "CONFEDERATE."

When Grant had Vicksburg besieged with dread,
And the two great armies frowned,
Keen sentries paced in their measured tread,
    With step undaunted,
    Where both flags flaunted
On hills with batteries crowned.

The sentry walked on his silent beat;
"Halt! Halt! and who goes there?"
A little girl paused, nor made retreat.
    But raised her hand
    As this command
Rang out on the clear, night air.

"Don't speak so loud! you man with a gun,
You certainly can not fear
A little girl, such a tiny one,
    That's just come through
    To see if you
Had some coffee over here."

"And where are you from, my little girl?"
"Yonder fort with cannons ten;
And I'll give to you this flaxen curl
    For coffee good,
    To fill my hood,
To take to my hungry men.

It's Texas Battery, Twenty-two,
And they have nothing to eat.
My papa was there until cut through
    By a cannon shot,
    From this very spot,
As reapers cut down the wheat.

"Your flag has more stripes and stars than ours;
Your coats are a pretty blue;
You've lots to eat—I've watched you for hours;
    My men would be glad,
    They said, if they had
Your food and tobacco, too.

"So I slipped away when no one knew,
And came down across the glen,
To beg some food of you 'Yanks' in blue;
    I know you'll be good,
    And fill my hood,
To take to my hungry men."

With best they had they loaded her down,
Those generous boys in blue.
"What lots of tobacco—it fills my gown!
    Here's each a kiss,
    And after this
I'll not let 'em shoot at you!"

"See here, Little Miss!" said gunner Drew,
"What was your father's name?
For it was my gun that cut him through!
    And I tell you what,
    'Twas a sorry shot,
But I, dear, was not to blame!"

"Don't feel so bad, Mr. Gunner man,
Or you'll set me cryin' again!
He's gone to heaven if any one can;
    For I've heard his prayer,
    To be taken there,
By the One who died for men.

I've been so lonely since he went away,
Up yonder to see my ma;
I'd never go back, if you'd let me stay;
    But sit on your lap,
    Mr. Gunner chap,
For you look just like my pa.

My papa's name? What's the matter with you,
You've grown so awfully pale?
His name was Captain John Gailord Drew!
  The gunner moaned!
  The gunner groaned!
"My God! 'Twas my brother 'Gail'!"

Those batteries roared like heaven's thunder—
When battle was on next day;
  While Vicksburg tumbled—
  And Pemberton grumbled—
And wounded found time to pray;
  One victory more—
  Our flag floated o'er
Rebellion's banner now torn asunder;
  And fields were red
  With dying and dead—
Thus battles are won, they say—
Those gunners saw, with silent wonder,
  Their little 'Confed.'
  Lead Uncle Ed
To that grave just over the way,
  Where tears of the Blue
  The earth soaked through,
Till they wet the face of the Gray!

THE MUTILATED SOLDIER.

When Billy Gardner went to war
   He wept to that degree,
His sweetheart, Minnie, said he'd best.
   Go with the *infant-ry!*

He said: My dear, be faithful,
   And I'll be true to you;
And write love-letters often;
   She said: "O, *billet-deaux.*"

His ear was shot off in the fight:
   He scampered to the rear,
And said a ball came whistling
   A little bit *tune-n-ear.*

A comrade said: When sweetheart hears
   She'll not have you at all:
Or say she *can-non* other love,
   Then have a *Minnie-bawl.*

He next was wounded in the side,
    His blouse with gore was wet;
He said: 'tis but dyspepsia—
    I have a *bayon-et*.

And when the wound was quite healed up
    He'd oft point to the scar,
And claim the port hole in his side
    Made him a *man-o'-war*.

A mortar shell took off a leg—
    "O, Doctor, must I die?"
"Not yet," the kindly surgeon said—
    "Unless it *mortar-fy*."

Pray, comrades, send a message home,
    By quick *te-leg-raphy;*
And give my love this *boon*, my last
    And only *leg-I-see*.

I hoped to make an officer,
    And ride about in saddle—
Ambition's lost its chiefest prop;
    They've shot off half my *straddle*.

You're late at drill, the Captain said:
    I can't *mark-time*, said he;
And if I use my gun for crutch
    A stand of arms I'll be.

One half my understanding's gone;
    What's left I'll try to save;
And yet there's precious little hope
    With one leg in the grave.

Both arms went off: *disarmed* at last
He cried: War hath no charms;
Kind comrades, pick these members up,
    And help me *shoulder-arms.*

To arms! I cried when war broke out;
    Then arms were furnished free;
And now I cry again in hopes
    Two-arms they'll furnish me.

I'm fit for naught in war or peace,
    Save Senate Hall debate;
I might succeed in politics,
    For I can *stump* the State.

A bullet next took out an eye;
    He ran with all his might,
And swore he'd never fight again,
    But keep well *out-of-sight.*

I am not cross-eyed, now, he said,
    For one's an empty socket;
I'll keep one eye upon the foe,
    The other in my pocket.

The Mutilated Soldier.

They found him sleeping on his post;
    He answered with a sigh:
The charge is false, dear Captain, for
    I only closed one eye.

Last night you stationed me out there
    To guard the " *U. S. A.*,"
And closely watch—when you know well
    I can not " *C. S. A.*"

You are too blind, the Captain said;
    You must examined be:
I am content, he then replied,
    For I'll be marked " *I. C.*"

A saber cut upon the scalp
    Soon solved this warlike riddle:
He'll be a *dude* forevermore:
    His hair parts in the middle.

The Captain said, with quiet grace:
    My ranks you now deform;
You must not come on *dress parade*
    Till you're more *uniform*.

At Roll Call answered thus his name:
    To truth I must adhere;
More than a quarter absent, sir;
    Not quite three quarters here.

When war was done they all went home
    He caught his Minnie's eye,
And said: the war is broken up,
    And so indeed am I.

And when he asked her if she'd wed,
    She answered with a laugh,
And said: "I've *half* a notion, sir,
    But want the *other half*.

I would assuredly, she said,
    Accept you with impunity;
But fear you are not able to
    Embrace the opportunity.

I promised once to marry you,
    She said, with smile quite bland;
Pray tell me, should I take your heart
    Unless I get your hand?

'Twould be an outrage, sir, indeed,
    To rob one so bereft;
For, should I take away your heart
    You'd have so little left.

How shall we manage if we're wed,
    You have so little pelf?
Can you support a wife while you
    Can not *support* yourself?

I'll marry you, but still I fear
   'Twill make my friends all laugh
To hear me introduce you as
   My *all*, my better *half*.

There's one plan will support us well;
   'Tis all you're fitted for:
Go in a Dime Museum as
   A relic of the war.

When asked if he had been to war
   He answered, quick; you bet;
And if I'm not mistaken, friends,
   The most of me's there yet.

When ladies decorate the graves
   This courtesy is shown:
They give him flowers, and bid him go
   And decorate his own.

POTOMAC!

Delivered at 17th Annual Reunion of the Society of the Army of the Potomac, San Francisco, August 2, 1886.

All hail to the North ! and all hail to the South !

Nations only are born at the cannon's mouth !
There is sometimes a rain, and there's sometimes a drouth,
   And there's sometimes a flood,
   When the land swims in blood;
. But there's no stronger Union a people may know
Than a Nation cemented by life's crimson flow.

When the great slumb'ring guns of old Sumpter awoke,
And clamored Rebellion in first battle smoke,
   The great North heard the cry
   Echoed back from the sky !
On learning its import, at first they were dumb !
Then shouted: " 'Tis war ! Be it so ! Let it come ! ! "

An army sprang up as the storm comes at sea ;
Or the peace-ladened air, when the winds are set free !
   Gath'ring fury anon,
   This fierce cyclone moved on—
Till down went the foes of this heaven-cherished Nation !
And Slavery lay buried 'neath wild desolation.

The miner has left his rich ledge in the gorge!
The fire has gone out at the old smithy forge—
    And the apron lies down
    On the anvil's bright crown,
And the helper no more hears the hammer's alarm!
For there's much sharper steel in the smith's brawny arm.

Left to rust is the scythe in the half-mown swath!
While the tailor, rigged out in new government-cloth,
    Never fails to make bruit
    Of his ready-made suit!
And the "cap" takes the place of the farmer's broad brim,
For he's turned from the furrow that turns oft from him!

Comes the hunter from out the wild haunts of the stag!
'Cause he heered how that some one had fired on the flag!
    If they'd tell him the name
    He'd go huntin' that game—
With his old-fashioned rifle, but no haversack!
He'd be durned if he'd carry *that* thing on his back!

The mother stands waiting that youth from the bank;
She clings to his neck as he walks to the rank—
    And his cheeks are still wet
    Where their hot tears have met!
But useless the tears that make mother-eyes red,
When a youth by his country's fair Goddess is led!

And yet they keep gathering and marching away !
Has the Nation turned soldier—and all in a day ?
    There's the father and son !
    While the miller takes gun,
With the dust of the wheat still whitening his hair !
Pray, where are they going, with this martial air ?

In solid battalions—a 'thrice armed' fate—
They go, this great question to arbitrate,
    With their glittering steel
    And the gun's rumbling wheel :—
Shall the old Stars and Stripes be forbidden to fly
In the land of its birth, it has hallowed for aye ?

Up from the South, with the trappings of war,
Came Chivalry dragging a Juggernaut car !
    In its progress of woe
    Crushing both friend and foe !
While the blood of the victims bespattered the guise
Of Slavery—Moloch of sacrifice !

Two millions of men, by opinions estranged !
By shedding of blood shall opinions be changed ?
    Let brothers remain,
    And opinions be slain !
Brave Southrons, pray put that strange banner aside !
And save this great Nation its first fratricide !

You will not? Then strike the hoarse tocsin of war!
And opinion abide with the Conqueror!
    On the banks of Bull Run
    The great conflict begun!
And out ran the life-wine, in crimson libation;
While on rushed the stream with its red irrigation!

On the banks of the Rapidan, stretching away,
In a low, tangled forest, ambushes the "Gray";
    Covered up, as with cloak,
    By the thick, scraggy oak!
Down there in the "Wilderness" fight they with Lee,
As Pharaoh's host struggled in the Red Sea.

The cannon are useless—those chariots of steel—
As the war-carts of Pharaoh, wanting a wheel.
    No cavalry rush
    Through the pine and the brush!
Yet Potomac's brave infantry wade through the flood
Of crimson dyed foliage—Red Sea of blood!

At Cold Harbor, when ordered to second attack,
With names writ on paper and pinned to their back—
    Death's authentic clue—
    Went those brave boys in "blue"
To battle, determined to conquer or die
With their face to the dust and their back to the sky!

Down the ranks Glory strides, thus labeling her dead
With her own autograph, just a few hours ahead !
  Tears rained from the skies,
  Ruing such sacrifice;
Like the Christ walking Calvary bearing his cross;
While Pity walked after, lamenting the loss.

Sweet Goddess of Liberty, never know fear !
No power on earth conquers thy volunteer !
  Fighting on while they bled
  O'er the enemy's dead—
Was a deed of such desperate courage sublime—
Like the "Charge of Six Hundred"—'twill live to all time !

At the first of the siege—in an old Richmond church—
Jeff Davis was knelt in religious research,
  When a shell struck the steeple,
  And frightened the people !
He stopped his devotions, beginning to swear,
On learning the devil had answered his prayer !

He rushed out bewildered, like one at a fire,
And grabbed up his step-mother's kitchen-attire !
  There was no other plan
  For this versatile man—
And the chief of that quondam Confederation
To mademoiselle made a quick transformation.

Jeff thought to escape through the long Union line,
In bustle and hoops and a loose crinoline;
    But the wicked old flirt
    Kept raising the skirt;—
Till the soldiers observed, as she ambled and skirred,
This doughty old woman was *booted and spurred!*

To Middleto'n, southward, from Winchester town,
A black horse, with Sheridan, comes dashing down!
    On the back of that steed
    Sits the one man they need!
He's "twenty"! he's "fifteen"! he's "ten"! miles away!
Another "five" miles, and he's right in the fray!

Who ever dare claim that the Southrons ride ill!
For they rode passing well at old Fisher's Hill!
    In that great steeple-chase,
    Called the "Woodstock Race,"
Phil. Sheridan rode, but the Rebels who fled
Came under the wire just a good neck ahead!

How fiercely they rode! 'Twas a terrible canter
Like the Phantom-chased ride of young Tam O'Shanter!
    With feet in the gyves,
    They rode for their lives;
For they heard on the wind, such demoniac laughter,
They knew either Phil. or the devil was after!

Lee thought that "Five Forks" in a road were too many,
And starting off cross-lots, he didn't take any,
        For he said: "I'll cut through!"
        Phil. said: "D———d if you do!"
Lee first thought he would, and then thought he wouldn't;
The fact that he didn't was proof that he couldn't!

No hero e'er conquered a more stubborn foe;
And never did captor such courtesy show
        As Grant did to Lee;
        This was his decree:
"Let officers freely retain their side arms,
And soldiers their horses for tilling the farms!"

One could conquer the world with such retinue:
A phalanx of patriots—brave boys in blue!
        This great leader thought
        No army e'er fought
So bravely! Each soldier a true volunteer!
Each soldier a freeman! Each soldier his peer!

The palm, unto him, must all history yield
Who ne'er lost a battle and never a field!
        While Potomac's great host
        Of this glory may boast:—
By the world-honored Grant our great army was led!
Immortal his fame: though Ulysses be dead!

Antietam, Ball's Bluff, Seven Oaks, Malvern Hill,
Spottsylvania, Fredericksburg, Chancellorsville,
      Petersburg, Cedar Creek,
      Where Early grew meek!
But the list of your battles can never be known
Till we count every drop and record every groan.

Mankind never waged such a conflict before!
Better foemen ne'er met in the battles of yore!
      No stamp on their faces
      Showed unequal races;
But brothers in valor, in gallantry, yea,
E'en brothers in blood were the Blue and the Gray!

The high-mettled Southron, undaunted and brave,
That strange three-barred banner would bear to his grave.
      But he'd win in the fight!
      For he thought he was right!
And it took the best blood from the palace, the cot,
And the tears and the cypress to prove he was not!

And these were the foemen you met in the fray!
And these were the foemen who oft barred your way—
      Going down to a man,
      In the great caravan
That went to eternity rather than yield!
There's carnage in battle when valor's a-field!

Was victory easy? Did their ranks subside
As the marsh-reeds go down with the rush of the tide?
   You should have been down
   At Gettysburg town
Where Meade fought with Lee! 'Twas the battle of *men!*
Had Meade been defeated—pray tell us—what then?

Lee brought Eighty Thousand and knocked at the gate!
While Meade thundered back in the round-shot debate!
   In three days the slain
   So covered the plain
A National graveyard was made of the field!
We'll call it "God's acre"—for he took the yield!

While Sherman's great army went thund'ring afar—
Potomac's battalions were strangling red war!
   Thus they fought! thus they bled!
   Till Slavery fell dead
At famed Appomattox, and sank to her grave,—
Close wrapped in the flag that's forbidden to wave!

Then our eagle came down from the ramparts of heaven—
Where our banner's great archetype proudly is driv'n,—
   Where the sun makes the bars,
   And where God fixed the stars,
In that grand Union Jack of perpetual blue—
On his outstretched wings bearing a *blessing to you!*

A blessing from heaven, where Freedom has birth ;
As the blessing of Bethlehem came to the earth
    On a bright Christmas morn,
    When the Savior was born ;
Such *Peace and Good Will* to the world bringing then,
That centuries after we still sing: *Amen ! !*

The grandest of nations the world ever knew
Would then have been severed, brave men, but for you !
    While the dead in the breach
    Forever shall teach :—
This Union must stand as our forefathers gave it !
And when 'tis assailed there are brave sons to save it !

The bayonet, flattened, has turned to a spade ;
A capital scythe is the old saber blade;
    With the same martial strain,
    Through the rich, golden grain,
The veteran whistles while cutting his way,—
Recalling war's harvest of Blue and of Gray.

The plowman is humming a mournful refrain,
While thinking of furrows they made for the slain.
    When the battle was over,
    And laid 'neath the clover,
Down there in the trenches long, dead files of men
The great Judgment spade shall uncover again.

The Southron is tilling, with sad, sun-brown face,
Those acres enriched by the blood of his race!
      On the grave of his foes
      And his kindred, he sows;
While the roots of the vine take their life from the dead,
And the wine of the vineyard forever is red.

Two teamsters have paused in the shade of the pool,
Rehearsing the tricks of the old army mule!
      They have little to say
      Of the Blue and the Gray
Which they wore when the garments meant shedding of
          blood—
They're discussing the mule and "Virginia mud."

The farmer is planting the corn in the row;
His boy and his gun have the best of the crow;
      The boy—he may die!
      The crow—he may fly!
That old army gun is a treacherous toy,
And may get the best of the crow and the boy!

There's a smile on the face of yon tailor, I note,
For a neighbor has brought him an old army coat;
      The thing has been torn!
      The thing has been worn!
From long force of habit, with suspicious air,
He raises the collar to see *what* is there!

As far distant hills take the atmosphere's hue,
So the Gray of Rebellion appears to be blue;
    And those who were foes
    Are now changing clothes—
The ranks of the veterans are fading away—
And those who wore Blue—are they not wearing Gray?

We honor the living—forget not the dead—
For e'en little children lay flowers on their bed
    To perfume their sleep;
    While fond mothers keep
Still watching for boys who will never return—
Though the lamp of remembrance at each casement burn·

They sleep on the hillside—they bivouac the glades;
The grass standing sentry with soft saber blades!
    Where the wild flower blooms
    Are their banner-wrapped tombs;
Fond Nature pays homage to valor like this,—
While the Nation drops flowers—and heaven drops a kiss!

Comrades of Potomac—O, where are the rest?
With *cartridge-made buttons* * sunk deep in each breast,
    In grave-faded Blue,
    At Death's grand Review,
With erstwhile commanders, on yon distant shore
Of heaven's fair Potomac, they march evermore!

  * Referring to the custom of Veterans wearing a button-badge made of copper from the empty shells gathered on the battle field.

They're guarding their *Capital City* on high ;
Their Camp-fires burn brightly for you, in the sky !
      There's a faith that assures
      Their old countersign, yours !
That man who for Country and Liberty dies
Needs no further passport, methinks, to the skies !

INDEPENDENCE DAY.

Delivered at San Francisco, July 4th, 1886.

THE FIRST KNOWN YANKEE NOTION.

In days of old, certain patriots bold,
   When England grew pedantic,
Unfurled to the gale the Mayflower's sail
   And ferried o'er the Atlantic.

On Plymouth rock was landed the stock
   With modest oriflamb
Who framed the state we perpetuate,
   Entitled our *Uncle Sam.*

Our freedom achieved, was there conceived,
   The first known " Yankee notion,"
Of the " Lion" born and the " Unicorn,"
   But on this side the ocean.

The infant grew, as infants do,
   Into a youthful nation;
When the English yoke began to choke
   And it cried for emancipation.

Then England thought, as England ought,
    We're losing by relaxation;
We'll keep them down by oppression's frown
And the grinding heel—*taxation.*

So she sent o'er the sea a cargo of tea,
    With a deal more tax than cargo;
Which so raised the ire of the patriot sire
    He placed on that ship his embargo.

Those patriots old, so we are told,
    Didn't like *tax* in their tea;
So they threw it away in Boston Bay,
    For the mermaids down in the sea.

Then John Bull came across the main
    To stop this Yankee row;—
He cared not a jot for the patriot—
    He's more respectful now.

But Washington George, the man in charge,
    Before he began to strike,
Held up his saber and said: " Kind neighbor,
    Whichever end you like."

And what, think you, was his choice of the two?
    This stubborn English *John*
Preferred the blade—the mistake he made
    Was proved to him anon.

They served him right on Charleston height;
  Like the story of "Jack and Gill,"
He came tumbling down and broke his crown,
  At the foot of Bunker Hill!

Like herds of cattle they came into battle,
  At Lexington, Monmouth, Yorktown;
But always, 'tis said, they dropped their bread,
  Which fell with the butter side down.

His lordship fine thought he would dine
  On Yankee tenderloin—
But the very first fight took the appetite
  And the sword of this Lord Burgoyne.

So one hot July day John Hancock did say
  To a large continental attendance;
I've a Yankee notion to make a motion
  For Declaration of Independence.

I thought about writing one out
  In the form of a "Thanatopsis";
'Tis too long, indeed, for one to read,
  So I'll give you a short synopsis.

When, in human events, with good intents,
  Two nations are tired of sticking;
If one has the grit to make the split,
  There's no use in the other's kicking.

We may be the scion of the " British Lion "—
But listen to my harangue:—
The American *crow* will let 'em know
We can run our own *shebang*.

This striped rag is our own flag,
And floats in our own breezes;
And England may stay across the *Bay*
And do as she "*durned*" pleases.

That great Declaration made by the nation
Tells the reason why,
With great demonstration and more perspiration,
We celebrate Fourth of July.

OUR COUNTRY.

He who bears not the love of his country at heart
On some desert should dwell, from his fellows apart;
Where the voice of no mortal, the song of no bird,
Nor even the cry of the jackal is heard;
Where his footstep falls hushed in the dry, yielding sand,
To plod on alone in a sun-blistered land;
With no living thing with which to converse;
For his heart is a desert, his being a curse.

Who loves not his country loves not his God;
His soul feeds on treason, rebellion and fraud.
'Tis better for him that he dwell off, alone,
Where silence oppresses life's dull monotone;
Or, far better still, since created in scorn,
This lep'rous nonentity had not been born.

We honor that man, where'er he may roam,
Who still loves his country next to his home,
And sings from his heart this great National song:

We honor the Russian who plods through the snow
"*My Country forever! Be she right or wrong!*"
To fight for his flag, though the world be his foe.

And the Turk, in the land that Mahommet has giv'n,
Whose cimeter curves like the crescent in heaven.

We honor the German who holds as divine
His great country's goddess, his loved "*Wacht am Rhine.*"

All hail to Great Britain! that land of renown!
On whose mighty kingdom the sun goes not down!
In the great world of waters there's no breeze nor gale
But pushes her commerce or stretches her sail.—
Where enterprise carries the great English tongue
Old lands become new, aged nations grow young.

And who does not love this great country of ours,
Where the blessings of heaven come down with the show'rs
That moisten the roots of that fruit-bearing tree
Our forefathers planted and called *Liberty* ;
Whose branches spread out with a foliage vernal—
A century's growth proving its life eternal?

On the *North* the stern ice-king stands guard in the snow;
From the South at the tropics the mild zephyrs blow,
All ladened with perfume that sweetens the air,
Like censers at church, when the Nation's at prayer.

Huge mountains, piled up, guard the broad Western shore
With its famed *Golden Gate*, where the sun is the door
That drops in the ocean to let us go through
On our pathway to heaven! Don't it seem so to you?

At the East, where the waves of Atlantic are hurled,
Stands our *'Liberty-statue,'* *' Enlightening the World'* ;
Her mute lips uttering the law written there
On her tablet of stone, lifted high in the air ;
As the words of Jehovah from Moses' lips fell
At Sinai's mountain to great Israel ;
Like the " pillar of fire," that torch in her hand
Lights the people of God to this fair promised land.
This tribute from France stands at Liberty's door,
A token of friendship, a bond evermore!
And we say to the land of the famed Lafayette,
When the world turns to ashes, 'twill be standing yet!

As the great poet said: " All the world is a stage " ;
So in consummate acting all nations engage.
Sometimes a fierce tragedy takes the play,
More often 'tis comedy—laugh as you may :—
While old " Uncle Sam," along with the rest,
To amuse the queer public is doing his best.

Though Russia lays claim to a very large map,
Her soldiers are frozen with every cold snap;
She keeps working South without leave or law—
She wants to get down where the nation can thaw ;—
To enlarge her dominion? No! No! That's all " *bosh* "—
'Tis warm water she needs, so the soldiers can wash.

At enormous expense France is fighting Tonquin ;
It's the toss of a copper which language will win.

We suggest arbitration between these great pow'rs;
If France wants the Chinese she can come and take ours;
And we'll throw in a statue, much bigger, more lasting,
That will put in the shade this Bartholdi's great casting.

Baby Greece has been trying to pick up a row
With the Old man of Turkey—but didn't know how;
When all the big nations with navies so stern
Came 'round and *boycotted* the little concern.

Old Bismark sits there in a mezzanine box,
Close watching the play, with the eye of a fox;
His part of the programme, as he understands,
Is furnishing orchestras, raising brass bands;
But somehow he never allows them to use
China-fiddle, nor *bag pipe,* nor *harp of the Jews.*

De Lesseps—first comedian—strides through the play;
His part is to dig the great *Isthmus* away;
But such is the death-rate he can't get ahead,
For most of his digging is graves for the dead.
Yet still the great Frenchman keeps diggin' and *hopin'*
There'll come a great earthquake and burst the thing open.

Old England's a-broil with her " Home Rule " jars,
About " wearing the green "—like the Hayes Valley cars.
To the " tight little Island " it's worse than a drug,
To take " Irish whiskey" from a *Glad-stone jug.*

In Ireland, 'tis said, pedagogues at the school
Whip all the small boys with the English Home Rule.

While our own President is too busy of late,
With the newly annexed matrimonial state,
To attend to our troubles—as most people wish:
The Chinese, Apaches and mackerel fish—
With our fishing smacks captured in Canada's tide—
He, too, takes a *smack* by kissing the bride.

If Canada's *rude* we'll have to "out flank 'er"—
And take with the fish every renegade *banker*.

And what with Apaches we've trouble enough,
Who wear out our soldiers at " Blind man's Buff."
But where they are now no one seems to know,
Not even their cousins in Old Mexico.

Great America, hail! summer fallow of God,
Where Liberty's breeze stoops to kiss the green sod.
From the north to the Gulf-land, from ocean to ocean,
Thy sons worship thee with patriot devotion.
From the earth to the blue vault of heaven away,
Rises up the grand anthem of Freedom to-day.
Thine eagle spreads out his broad wings in the air,
All laden down withthe nation's prayer,
And soars up aloft through the blue vault and all,
Till he perches at last on eternity's wall;

Up through the blue ether no mortal has trod,
His charge laying down at the throne of God.

As bulwarks of freedom, defiantly stand
Thy mountains plowed up by the Almighty's hand.
Thine oceans stretch out from either shore,
A safeguard perpetual forevermore.

No servile soldiers defend thy broad realm;
No heavy crowned monarch sits at thy helm;
Thy soldiers are sons from the anvil, the plow,
They stand ever ready, they're ready e'en now,
To gather by millions in battle array,
From the North, from the South, both the " Blue and the Gray."

No incision so deep by sharp, saber steel,
But the *Amor Patriae* always will heal.

The " Blue and the Gray" are in battle no longer,
Fierce war has cemented their brotherhood stronger.

Ere the war-trumps last echo had died away,
Or chaplain to God could his orisons say,
With shouts of thanksgiving for battle release,
Both armies returned to the arts of peace.
History gives us no parallel case,
For every soldier returned to his place.

'Twas American purely, a God-given dower,
And therein consists this nation's great power.
No standing army guards mountain and dell;
Each man guards his own and improves it as well;
For all the army this nation can boast
Is a few scattered squads like the frontier post;
Not intended as safeguards of the nation
But as chaperones to a Reservation,
Whose duty it is to keep, no doubt,
Not the Indians in, but the citizens out.
But once let war's clarion notes be rung,
Like a frenzied tigress, mad for her young,
From the North, from the South, from either shore
They'll gather by millions, and millions more,
And then (I speak with more pride than vanity)
America defies all the rest of humanity.

Great America, hail! summer fallow of God,
Where Liberty's breeze stoops to kiss the green sod,
Thy resources boundless by bounty divine,
In the gold of the harvest and gold of the mine.
Industry keeps thee ahead of thy neighbor;
While thrift wins thee more than the bullet or saber.

Mountain and stream divide brother from brother;
They bridge the one and tunnel the other.
They polished the shaft and adjusted the wheel,
And the great iron horse all a-glitter with steel,

Drags through the mountain and over the plain,
Humanity freighted, the long, rumbling train.

Who thought the light'ning would ever inspire
Life in the veins of a slender wire?
Yet they belted the globe and threaded the sea,
And the quickened tongue of the telegraph key
To the listening ear now whispers the thought
On a delicate wire from antipodes brought.

To claim all the glory is not our intention,
Yet everything new seems a Yankee invention.
This Yankee, distinctive, is of strange formation,
You find his like in no other nation;
He's lean and slender, he's lank and tall,
And speaks with a sort of elongated drawl;
The *dogondest critter* that ever one sees,
And always a-gettin' *new-fangled idees.*
There ain't no enterprise you can mention,
That he *haint* tried with some invention.
If the world's ever blest with *perpetual motion*,
I'll bet ten to one it's a *Yankee notion.*

America rests in the ocean's broad arms!
Not lured to her slumber by siren's charms;
But the rocking of billows on either shore,
And the waves' lullaby sung to her evermore.
Forever and aye shall her glory increase,
While the ocean keeps singing this anthem of peace.

Were I, great nation, to give thee a toast,
This would I say, without idle boast ;—
"Land of the freeman, to Liberty giv'n
The pride of the earth and the favored of heaven,
Broken from Europe by thunderbolts hurled—
Shoved out in mid-ocean to balance the world!
When 'Father Time' writes thine epitaph
The world's great glory is lessened by half."

APOSTROPHE TO THE EAGLE.

Fear not, grand eagle,
The bay of the beagle!
No hunter his gun will incline!
He's branded with shame
Whoever takes aim
At thy freedom, a right divine!

Great bird, thou art king
Of all that bear wing!
And this was thy country of old!
'Way back in creation,
Before 'twas a Nation,
Or known to Columbus, the bold.

With the red man's, primeval,
Thy birthright's coeval,
By Deity given in feoff!
'Twas not his war bonnet,
But thy plumage on it,
Made the crown of the old Indian Chief!

Like the dove to the ark—
That ancient bark,
When the world was deluged for sin—
Flying out on the sea
To greet Liberty,
And pilot the Mayflower in!

The sunset red
On the white clouds shed
Made stripes for our Goddess divine :—
While she stitched the bars,
You brought down the stars,
That completed the grand design.

'Twas thy sweeping wing
Did the first breath bring
To the sail of the great " Constitution " :
While from first to last
You wheeled 'round her mast,
In the smoke of the old Revolution.

When those men in " Gray "
Tore three stripes away
From that flag by our forefathers given,
'Twas thy piercing call
Made the thunderbolt fall,
By which fierce Rebellion was riven.

Start not from thy poise
At that rumbling noise,
When the lightning and storm disagree;
It is not a battle,
'Tis only the rattle
Of heaven's artillery.

From thine eyrie, the crag,
Watch over thy flag,
And ne'er let it trail in the dust!
Soaring high in the air
Ever this ægis bear:
" *In Freedom, and God is our Trust.*"

Fear not, grand eagle,
The bay of the beagle!
No hunter his gun will incline!
He's branded with shame
Whoever takes aim
At thy freedom, a right divine!

www.ingramcontent.com/pod-product-compliance
Lightning Source LLC
Chambersburg PA
CBHW031401160426
43196CB00007B/851